YOUR KNOWLEDGE HAS

Bibliographic information published by the German National Library:

The German National Library lists this publication in the National Bibliography; detailed bibliographic data are available on the Internet at http://dnb.dnb.de .

Imprint:

Copyright © 2016 GRIN Verlag, Open Publishing GmbH
Print and binding: Books on Demand GmbH, Norderstedt Germany
ISBN: 9783668420281

This book at GRIN:

http://www.grin.com/en/e-book/354868/big-data-powering-the-next-industrial-revolution

Swaroop Gayam

Big Data. Powering the Next Industrial Revolution

GRIN Publishing

GRIN - Your knowledge has value

Since its foundation in 1998, GRIN has specialized in publishing academic texts by students, college teachers and other academics as e-book and printed book. The website www.grin.com is an ideal platform for presenting term papers, final papers, scientific essays, dissertations and specialist books.

Visit us on the internet:

http://www.grin.com/

http://www.facebook.com/grincom

http://www.twitter.com/grin_com

Big Data: Powering the Next Industrial Revolution

BY

Swaroop Reddy Gayam

Applied Research for Technology

Date: 11/27/2016

UNIVERSITY OF CENTRAL MISSOURI

Big Data: Powering the Next Industrial Revolution

Abstract:

The word Big Data not just refer to large data sets but also includes frameworks and tools used to analyze the data. Every day hundreds of Gigabytes data has been flooded from various sources like social media, healthcare, public utility, and search engines. Every bit of data following is important and will be stored. With this type of technology collection of data is not a problem but the dark hidden problem with this immense data is most of the data collected is in unstructured form. It is very difficult to analysis this uncertain data called data deluge, this the major problem faced by big data. This paper talks about how to overcome this problem and talk about the importance of big data, the complexity involved in analyzing big data need of big data to overcome business concerns and new techniques to analysis big data

Table of Contents:

INTRODUCTION

Information today has gone from scarce to superabundant which brings immense new benefits but complementary big headache too. With the rapid development of Internet of things, cloud computing, and mobile Internet, the rise of Big Data has attracted increasingly concern, which brings not only great benefits but also crucial challenges on how to manage and utilize Big Data better. In my paper, I would like discuss the application of Big Data in various verticals and this article examines the opportunities and concerns over big data in various felid. The term "BIG DATA" was given by Roger Magoulas from O'Reilly media in 2005. He explained that due to its whopping size and complexness, wide range of data sets is almost becoming insoluble to handle and manage through traditional data management tools. Big data can be seen in Banking and business for Inventory Management, Customer Behavior, and Market Behavior. Big data is also seen in life sciences for analyzing and advance research in Genome sequencing, clinical data and patient data areas. Big data could also be seen in other areas like Astronomy and Oceanography (Buchel, 2015).

What is Big data and how is it changing the way researchers in companies and other organizations are learning about the world around them. From where do these data come and how it's being processed. What big data means to the real world and what are the results obtained at the end, these are all such queries that strike our mind when we think of big data.

It is not known what size of database is considered or referred to be big but Big data is defined as the tools that are needed to process it to use this big data programs are to be written such that they can span multiple physical/virtual machines working together in order to process all of the data in short span of the time (Menichelli, 2015).

It needs special techniques to write the programs that can produce perfect result from different machines related with each other and then integrate the whole pool of results. It is faster to access the data using a program that is stored locally compared to when it is over a network, so the distribution of the data across cluster and how the networking is done is also important when we think about big data problems (Menichelli, 2015).

Statement of Problem:

Today every bit of data is important and hence stored. The actual problem is that more the data more accurate analysis and forecast is possible but the dark truth behind it is that elephantine amount of uncertain data surrounds the actual data. This paper focuses on the biggest problem called data deluge, need of big data, application of big data, components of

4

big data, business intelligence versus big data analysis, business concerns in respect to big data, how big data overcomes the problems faced by business, techniques for analyzing big data, types of big data analysis, complex challenges for an organization to shift towards big data.

Purpose of Study:

This research was carried out to find the problem faced by the big data and find a solution. This paper also discusses the growing immense data is helpful in many verticals like insurance, healthcare, and many other businesses to draw more profits and provide better customer services. However, along with benefits, big data complementing with some problems that can be a headache for companies. In this research, the best possible solutions for these problems have been discussed.

The use of big data is replete with heightened security and privacy concerns. First, as big data accumulates at an unprecedented scale, along with our continual efforts in digitizing data, there is no shortage of concerns over how to store, process data while preventing those data from being abused or misused. A common misconception is when customers confuse the term Big Data with having to deal with lot of data. But the Truth is that volume is clearly a part of big data solution but Big Data is more about unlocking the potential of Structured & Unconstructed information, inside & potentially outside of our security system & doing it in right time.

Research Questions:

1. Why Big Data should matter to you?
2. Big Data is it a trouble or a real solution?
3. Understanding what is Big Data?
4. What are Components of Big Data?

Research Hypothesis

Null Hypothesis h0: Big Data is a big trouble

Alternative Hypothesis h1: Big Data is not a big trouble, it's a real solution.

Review of Current Literature

A key resource for the current economy is Information, which is not only renewable but also autogenic. Running out of it is not a problem but drowning into it is (Chopra & Madan, 2015).

Data deluge is a serious threat, for example, there is data every were with this enormous amount of data, in many cases we know that changes of data getting stolen, missing data, or even breached resulting in allowing illegitimate access to data. Research put forth the idea of avoiding these threats by understating the actual meaning of the big data. The unstructured data is like curd oil; unrefined data is valuable but cannot be used. Firstly, we need to process data and draw patterns for better insight; this will create the value for the data. User control can achieve this, giving the user the access to know about the data where it came and from whom it is shared. Taking the security issues seriously and conducting the security audits on a yearly basis will allow the companies to find the new threats, loopholes in the systems and make it more secure by taking preventive measures (Chopra & Madan, 2015).

This research was carried out to find the problem faced by the big data and find a solution. This paper also discusses the growing immense data is helpful in many verticals like insurance, healthcare, and many other businesses to draw more profits and provide better customer services. However, along with benefits, big data complementing with some problems that can be a headache for companies. In this research, the best possible solutions for these problems have been discussed.

Big Data: A Trouble or A Real solution

This paper deals with how do large amount of data is stored and what are the major threats that occur during this process. William Gibson once said that- "The future is here, but it's just not evenly distributed yet". The digital data grew from 1.2 zettabytes to 35 zettabytes and in 2011 there were 300 quadrillion files in which 90% of digital data was unstructured. As this is an alarming issue to solve this one must have in hand only the real data for it to be structured or processed, if there is so much of irrelevant data that is occupying the space then it should be disaffiliated (Chopra & Madan, 2015).

Alex Szalay, an astrophysicist at John Hopkins University, states that "The procreation of data is making them progressively unapproachable". In his view, everyone who is contributing to this never-ending data should know how to make sense of this data (Menichelli, 2015).

James Cortada of IBM said-"We are at a different period because of so much information." The data that is growing every day is being difficult to manage and tackle. Here the uncertain data is reproduced at a speed which is almost ten times larger than the real data (Chopra & Madan, 2015).

A real-time example discussed in the article was about the Wal-Mart which is a retail giant and it handles more than a million customers and their transactions every hour which is building up the databases approximately to more than 2.5 petabytes which is equivalent to 167 times more than the America's Library of congress. And, when we talk about Facebook it holds over 40 million photos and it keeps getting larger and larger. So, secure this large data it is already known that the conventional methods or techniques can't help the problem to solve so the scientists are working on advanced approaches which can manage and utilize this data (Chopra & Madan, 2015).

2.The Real Problem: Data Deluge

John Naisbitt quoted that-"we have for the first time an economy based on a key resource that is not only renewable, but self-generating. The Hazardous issue is the data deluge where in a lot of risk is associated, because this just data everywhere. So, to overcome the data deluge one must understand what big data is actually. Clive Humb and DUnn Humby says that "Data is the new oil. Data is just like crude. It's valuable, but if unrefined it cannot be really used. "So, the big data is what we are going to make out the data that which we have, so we need to create value first and then the pattern from that data to create an insight (Chopra & Madan, 2015).

This can happen when the following are done, they are

- Users must be given control, that is they must be given upper hand of their data and who can access it with various customizations allowed.

- Takin security issues seriously that is to control security breaches within the organizations they should start discussing and disclosing the security policies that are hidden now.

- Yearly examining security policies.

3.Why big data should matter to you?

The problem here doesn't lie in the acquisition of hefty data but the need of this data and when there is large amount of data then which is proportional to higher accurate analyses may lead to dauntless decision making (Buchel, 2015). So, study of big data is very much necessary and when the right decision is made it can help in resolving so many issues like: -

- It can extract the actual reason behind all the defects, flaws etc.

- Analyze millions of stocks keeping units

- Fully optimize the routes followed

- Customers with higher priority are recognized easily.

Advantages of Big Data

A Huge amount of data is not a problem; with more data, higher accuracy will be attained. With higher accuracy decision making in companies can be easily done. Ongoing growth of business using big data is a proof that companies need big data for more profits (Buchel, 2015). They are many ways Big data being used in present days to change our world, few of them are

- Understating the Customer needs which help in providing better service

- Optimizing business process for better growth and profits

- Used in health care, sports, education, and military applications

- Extensively used in science and research

- Improved security and used in law enforcement.

Lot of new opportunities and new jobs are created in industries in Big Data, In the figure below we can see 20 different industries offering jobs in Big Data.

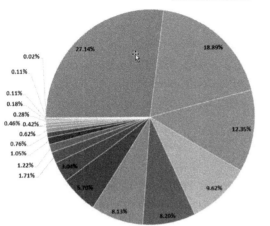

(Wanted analytics, 2014)

Figure 1: Big Data job opportunities in different industries.

Demand for Big data expertise has been widely increased over the past 1 year, there was 123% hike in the demand in the field information technology and over 89.8% increased demand in computer system.

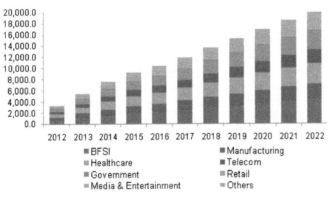

(Billore, 2015)

Figure 2: European market share of Big Data

9

Big Data help organization to improve their quality of managing large amount of information. Companies are using big data to provide better service to customers. In the above figure 2 we can see the market share of the big data in European market. It is expected that over 27 USD billion of business globally. However, it is very difficult to analysis this uncertain data called data deluge, this the major problem faced by big data. This paper talks about how to overcome this problem and also talk about the importance of big data. But the benefits of big data will overweigh the draw backs of the big data.

Methodology

Population

Population for this research is all industry that use Big Data in their operations. It may happen that I will not actually visit to industries to cover all industries in my study but I will cover as more as possible by going into internet sources. From internet, I will get news about any kind of issues companies facing by using Big data. I will make analysis of that and compare the advantages over disadvantages of big data. The application of big data is numerous, therefore taking random samples of problems from internet and using studies done by others will cover all areas and make this study more natural.

I will try to take examples of negative and positive side of big data. I have mentioned in my research topic. I will take at least one example for each of following. Because these are the main problem, industry is facing with Big data

- Huge data sets

- No proper tool to analysis big data sets

- Required advanced technology

- Challenges like social security and privacy issue

- Technology in wrong hands like terrorist, hacker etc.

- Lack of skilled big data engineers

- Companies need to change the complete system of storing and analyzing the data

If found different types of problem with same industry I will group as one and will analyses the situation accordingly. In addition, if same problem found in different industries will group them and make my analysis accordingly. This is to limit this study and not to make un-necessary studies of similar issues faced by organizations.

Instruments or apparatus used.

There are not as such any physical instrument to use to make this study. However, main tool to collect data and analyze is internet. Internet in terms of researches already conducted by researchers, news articles, actual newspapers, and company web pages. I also can choose one or two companies if I find some specific case or issue, they are facing big data management system. I will also find case studies in UCMO library for my study.

Internet source are good source because plenty of research work conducted by researchers is available to take and make my analysis. I will make analysis of big data problems faced by organizations and give suggestions on different issues. The main information I will be looking from each research work or case study is Big data advantages and disadvantages. I will look for information on how they handled that situation. It is same with case studies and newspaper articles.

Information collected from research work and case studies is valid and reliable. This is because those works are already in practice. They also have a list of reliable sources used for making that study. This makes it easy for me to believe that data and use that for my study. If I am taking some special case, I will collect data. I will use this data collected to make list of problems faces by using big data in their business and another list of how to handle those problems. And this problem can be acceptable over the advantages of using big data.

Statistical Analysis

For overall study, there is not data to make statistical analysis. However, one of my study about risks involved in using big data, I will rate all risk associated with using big data and will rank them from 1-5. After ranking, them from 1-5 I will take few example from my study and make a descriptive analysis to find which risk in more frequent than others risk and will write comment on mitigation strategy for each risk. The risk that have high frequency will have more concentration on writing mitigation strategy.

The advantage of using this software is we can investigate various patterns, able to identify trends in the given data. It can also evaluate statistical variables like mean, median, standard deviation, variance, and error. However, all this information, I will not use for conducting my analysis.

11

Any statistical analysis has following four steps.

Plan:

For making any statistical analysis, panning is necessary. Plan to collect data in my case; I will collect data from current and past research work done. As an output from this analysis, I will be looking for frequencies of each risk issues. It is ok to spend more time in planning as if we have full proof plan and contingency plan is in hand. This is because planning is base of nay study.

Collect:

Collection of data is done in this step. Different ways are there to collect data. Some of the data collection methods are observations, interviews, questionnaires, databases, samplings, or experimentations. However, as mentioned earlier I will collect data from research work done and real case studies conducted earlier. This are reliable data available on internet.

Process:

This step is to process the data collected in step two. I will take data and will conduct a descriptive analysis of different type of risks. Output from this will be frequency of each risk and a bar chart showing these frequencies will be important. A pie chart of all risk associated with big data will help to see percentage coverage of different risks.

Discuss:

Output received in process step is to be discussed in discuss step. The most frequent risk must be discussed in detail and the risk that are not so frequent and are special cases should be get separate attention.

Research Plan

Below are the steps to conduct my study.

- Define problem – Big Data dark side and Bright side
- Collect related research works, case studies and newspaper articles.
- Analyze collected data.
- Make a list of issues faced by Big data

- Make a list of different types of risks associated in using Big Data sets

- Rank all risks and overweigh them with advantages of Big data

- Make descriptive analysis of risks associated.

- Take output from descriptive analysis and make

- In details, make suggestions for mitigation strategies of risks.

- Overweighing advantages of big data

- Make a final document for research

Above are the summary of steps for conducting the research. In this research, the critical part is collecting data or information from research work done, case studies and newspaper articles. This is because intense research on internet should be done for collecting data.

Second important and critical thing is to make ranking of risks associated with big data. It may happen that the same risk is problem of most of the organizations. So finding different examples of different risk is a challenge. Again, for this intense research should be conducted on internet or find real case studies.

Third important part in this plan is making suggestion for mitigating risk associated in big data. For making suggestion for each type of risk and other issues with big data, a deep study of researched literature is necessary.

Time-on-Task Analysis:

This is main part of any research work or project. If researcher has perfect plan for each task and time allocated to each task it is easy for researcher to follow that plan. Researcher should stick to the plan and achieve all tasks on time it will be easy for him to finish the research on time.

For my purpose of this research, I have made one excel file (table) with describing each task and assigning time stamp for each task. This will help me in conducting this study on time and tracking my study at any time in research semester. It is a 10-week plan for conducting research.

Tasks to be done	WK1	WK2	WK3	WK4	WK5	WK6	WK7	WK8	WK9	WK10
Topic selection	■									
Defining Problem	■									
Questions to be answered		■								
Data collection		■								
Making List of Problems with Big Data			■							
Advantages of Big data			■							
Analysis				■						
Comparing Advantages and Disadvantages				■						
Suggest mitigation strategies					■					
Suggest solutions for other issues					■					
Final results						■				
Conclusion						■				
Documentation begins						■				
First draft							■	■		
Final draft									■	■

Table 1. - Time stamp for research work

14

Summary:

Companies continuously using this three factors user control, taking care of security breaches seriously in the organization and yearly examining security points are gaining more market initiative when compared to the companies which are not taking this measures to keep the transparency and giving freedom to the user. With this type of transparency user will have control over the data provided which is more secure and accurate data (Chopra & Madan, 2015).

Conclusion:

In this paper, the uses of big data and the need for big data analysis tool is clearly put forth. A Huge amount of data is not a problem; with more data, higher accuracy will be attained. With higher accuracy decision making in companies can be easily done. Ongoing growth of business using big data is a proof that companies need big data for more profits. However, companies should be able to outweigh the cons of big data over their pros.

Big Data help organization to improve their quality of managing large amount of information. Companies are using big data to provide better service to customers. In the above figure 2 we can see the market share of the big data in European market. It is expected that over 27 USD billion of business globally. This paper, talks about how companies overcome this problem and talk about the importance of big data. The benefits of big data completely overweigh the draw backs of the big data. My alternate hypothesis is correct.

Reference:

Billore, D. (2015, October 01). Big Data Market Size, Share | Industry Research Report, 2022. Retrieved from https://www.linkedin.com/pulse/big-data-market-share-forecasts-2022-grand-view-research-billore

Chopra, A., & Madan, S. (2015). Big data: A trouble or A real solution? International Journal of Computer Science Issues (IJCSI), 12(2), 221-229. Retrieved from https://login.cyrano.ucmo.edu/login?url=http://search.proquest.com/docview/1676820 866?accountid=6143

Columbus, L. (2015, May 25). Roundup of analytics, big data & business intelligence forecasts and market estimates, 2015. Retrieved from http://www.forbes.com/sites/louiscolumbus/2015/05/25/roundup-of-analytics-big-data-business-intelligence-forecasts-and-market-estimates-2015/#54f0134a4869

Columbus, L. (2014, December 29). Where big data jobs will be in 2015. Retrieved from http://www.forbes.com/sites/louiscolumbus/2014/12/29/where-big-data-jobs-will-be-in-2015/#5c51a952404a

Datafloq. (n.d.). Using Big Data to Target In-Market Shoppers. Retrieved from https://datafloq.com/read/using-big-data-target-in-market-shoppers/1052

Menichelli, F. (2015). The data revolution: Big data, open data, data infrastructures and their consequences. Surveillance & Society, 13(2), 319-321. Retrieved from https://login.cyrano.ucmo.edu/login?url=http://search.proquest.com/docview/1697734 047?accountid=6143

Fang, W., Zheng, Y., & Xiu, J. (2014). Big data: Conceptions, key technologies, and application. Nanjing Xinxi Gongcheng Daxue Xuebao, 6(5), 405-419. Retrieved from https://login.cyrano.ucmo.edu/login?url=http://search.proquest.com/docview/1622091 093?accountid=6143

Khan, N., Yaqoob, I., Ibrahim Abaker, T. H., Inayat, Z., Waleed Kamaleldin, M. A., Alam, M., . Gani, A. (2014). Big data: Survey, technologies, opportunities, and challenges. The Scientific World Journal,doi:http://dx.doi.org/10.1155/2014/712826

Buchel, O. (2015). Big data: A revolution that will transform how we live, work, and think. Journal of Information Ethics, 24(1), 132-135. Retrieved from https://login.cyrano.ucmo.edu/login?url=http://search.proquest.com/docview/1779996 183?accountid=6143.